Cross Reference
An innovative Bible marking system...

by
Dan Vis

Copyright © 2023 by Dan Vis
All rights reserved
including the right of reproduction
in whole or in part in any form.

All Scripture quotations are from the
King James Version of the Bible
Emphasis supplied unless otherwise indicated.

ISBN: 978-1-958155-07-3

Published by FAST Missions
111 2nd Street
Kathryn, ND 58049

Additional copies of this book are available by
visiting us at WWW.FAST.ST

Dedication

This book is dedicated to Yamil, Jeffrey, and Jay--three brothers who forever impressed me with just how cool Bible work really is. Thank you for your faithful, and radiant service.

Table of Contents

Day 1:   Be Ready Always. 1

Day 2:   The Basic Structure 6

Day 3:   Backup Verses 12

Day 4:   Sword Drills. 17

Day 5:   Expanding the System 23

Day 6:   Difficult Questions 28

Day 7:   Accelerated Sharing 32

Cross Reference
Preface

Looking back through the years, I can recall numerous times someone wanted to do a Bible marking class. The idea was simple: gather a long list of verses on some topic and then string them along together into a long chain--with each verse cross-reference to the next in their Bible. Then, move on to the next topic, and then the one after that. By the time you were finished, theoretically at least, you could find any verse you needed to answer a Bible question.

In reality though, it never really worked out all that well. What if you were studying with someone and they asked you a question that was best answered by verse #15 in that particular topic's chain? Were you really going to flip through 14 references to finally get to the one you needed? If you are looking for a system to help you answer people's questions, is this really the best solution?

In the pages ahead, I'm going to share with you a radically different approach to Bible marking designed deliberately to help you turn instantly to the exact verse you need to answer dozens of common Bible questions. And it's highly flexible, allowing you to add topics, and questions, and verses any time you like. In fact, I'll show you how to never be caught twice with the same objection unprepared.

The world these days is growing increasingly confused about what the Bible teaches. And people everywhere are looking for answers. Believers who know the truth, must determine to equip themselves to give those answers.

The innovative Bible marking system you are about to discover can help equip you to become one of those workers He can use.

Be Ready Always
Day 1

    Christians everywhere have a natural longing to share their faith with others. It's God-given. But all too often, we lack confidence in our ability to share. We fear we won't be able to find the verses we need to explain some perplexing topic. Or that someone will ask a question we can't answer. And so we hesitate. Life passes by, and friends pass on, while we stand there quietly, frustrated by our powerlessness to reach all but a few.
    But it doesn't have to be that way. This challenge can change things.
    In the days to come, you will discover an innovative Bible marking system you can use to answer questions to common Bible questions. Many chain referencing systems encourage you to link together a long chain of verses, one after the other. But what if you need the fifth verse in the chain, or the tenth—to answer a question? It's virtually impossible to get to the verse you need in any kind of normal witnessing situation. What's needed is a different approach.

Imagine now being able to turn to just the right verse to answer some challenging questions. And not just one or two questions, but dozens. It can happen. And we'll show you how.

There is much more to witnessing than just answering questions. But answering questions is an important part of witnessing. And it's a skill every believer should develop.

Follow the suggestions ahead, work at it for a while, and you'll soon be amazed at how your ability to answer questions has improved. And as your confidence grows, so will your commitment to sharing with others. And with increased commitment, God will be sure to send opportunities. He is not going to allow your efforts to equip yourself for service go unrewarded. You'll be well on your way toward becoming a worker.

And that's the urgent need of the hour, isn't it? More workers. The harvest is plenteous, but the laborers are few. Yes, every available person is needed. Jesus is soon to come, and untold millions are unprepared for what's ahead—as a result of either ignorance, or exposure to false teachings and distortions of Scripture. Now is the time to for men and women to rise up and share the truth!

To get ready for what's coming, I want to encourage you to take the first step, and select a Bible specifically for chain referencing. Choose one with as much margin space as possible. Also, try to find one with at least two or three blank sheets of paper in the back for notes. It's also helpful if it's not filled with lots of other markings already. If you don't have one handy, consider buying an inexpensive Bible just for this class. Once you have mastered the system, and gotten everything just how you want—you can copy your notes over to a nicer Bible at your convenience. Choose one for now to get started.

Ok, so much for today. Stay tuned till tomorrow when we begin introducing our "Cross Reference" Bible marking system.

Be Ready Always
Worksheet

How important is it to you, to be able to share your faith in response to people's questions?

What is the main problem with most Bible marking systems?

How would being able to turn to the exact verse people need increase your confidence in witnessing?

How important is it to mobilize as many workers as possible?

What things should you look for in choosing a Bible for this class?

Additional Notes:

The Basic Structure
Day 2

As we discussed yesterday, there is a great need today for men and women who know their Bibles, and can answer people's questions from it. But all too often, we lack confidence in our ability to answer questions, and as a result evade situations where we might have opportunity to share.

In the weeks to come, Cross Reference will help solve this problem. Most chain referencing systems link a long list of verses on some topic into a single long chain, making it difficult to find specific verses dealing with various aspects of that topic. Our approach collects clusters of questions on a topic, and then answers them with a few precise verses each. That way, when asked a specific question—you can turn straight to the verses you need! The paragraphs below will show you how.

In my experience, the latter approach is far more useful. If I need a long list of verses I can bring a printed study guide along. I want a Bible marking system that equips me to answer questions. That's the goal of the approach we're teaching here.

Building Blocks

Here are the basic building blocks of our cross reference system:

Bible Topics

It all begins with topics. Topics are broad categories around which you can collect clusters of questions. Suppose for example you want to be able to answer questions about the Bible itself. We might call that topic: "The Word of God." Each topic will need a "short-cut" word associated with it. In this case we could just use "Bible". Other broad topics might be the second coming, the law of God, or life after death. These topics help keep everything organized.

Clusters of Questions

A good topic serves as a focal point for a cluster of questions. With a topic like the Word of God, you might have questions related to how the Bible came into existence, whether or not it is inspired, how to study the Bible, the importance of memorization, and so on. If you can only come up with 1-2 questions, your topic may be too small. If you can think of a dozen questions or more, your topic may be too broad. Aim for somewhere in between!

Key Verses

Finally, each question should have one key verse answering it. This is the verse that most clearly and directly answers the question. For a question on inspiration, our best verse might be II Timothy 3:16. For a question on how to avoid deception, John 7:17 might be best. Many times there are multiple good verses, and I'll show you how to mark them in tomorrow, but for now you will have to limit yourself to just one verse per question.

Getting Started
   With this introduction, you are now ready to start in on your first topic. Here are the basic steps of our Cross Reference system in a nutshell:

1) Find a blank page in the back of the Bible and write "Bible Topics" at the top of the page.
2) Below it, write your first topic: "The Word of God".
3) Write out your key questions below it, with each preceded by your short-cut word, the question number, and the key verse.
4) Leave a little space below your last question in case you stumble across another common question later.
5) Repeat steps 2-4 for each topic you want to be able to answer questions about.

This is how this page might look after you complete your first topic:

Bible Topics

Word of God
BIBLE 1. How did we get the Bible? II Timothy 3:16
BIBLE 2. How can we know the Bible really is from God? Isaiah 46:9-10
BIBLE 3. Why is it important to study the Word of God? Joshua 1:8
BIBLE 4. How should we study the Bible? Acts 17:11
BIBLE 5. How can we avoid being deceived? John 7:17

   Now that you know what to do to get started, take a few moments to write out the first topic and its accompanying questions and key verses. We'll talk more about how to expand your system to chain reference additional topics in a future study. If you would like help coming up with additional topics, questions, and key verses, please see our Truth Corps class. It gives questions, key verses, and verse sets, on nearly 40 topics, plus much more information on sharing the Bible you will find extremely helpful.

Ok, this wraps up day two of our challenge. Tomorrow we'll talk about another essential feature of our Bible marking system: backup verses...

The Basic Structure
Worksheet

What should be the goal of a good Bible Marking system? How do many systems fail to achieve this?

What are the three building blocks used in our FAST Cross Referencing systems, and what is the purpose of each:

■

■

■

Show what it would look like to write out a topic on your "Bible Topics" page. Feel free to copy the example from the today's reading

Additional Notes:

Backup Verses
Day 3

Welcome back. So far we have talked about the urgent need for workers, and that one reason many don't witness is their lack of confidence in being able to answer people's questions. We've also looked at how a Bible marking system built on topics, questions, and key verses can equip us to answer questions more effectively.

And if you have completed the assignments for our first two days, you should have a Bible specifically for chain referencing, and at least one topic marked in on your Bible topics. Today we will talk about one more key ingredient in our Bible marking system.

Verse Lists

Jotting down the questions and a key verse for each is only the first step. Often there are several verses that could be used to help answer a question, or reinforce an answer. In fact, if you don't have several verses, you should be cautious. Building a doctrine on just one verse is dangerous! To give you rapid access to these backup verses, you will want to start marking in a "verse list" for each topic.

A verse list is simply a handful of verses you can use to supplement a key verse. In our example yesterday, our first question dealt with the issue of inspiration, and I suggested the key verse II Timothy 3:16. But that's certainly not the only verse on the subject. II Peter 1:21 describes the process of inspiration more fully. I Corinthians 2:13 looks at how God guides even in the selection of words. Psalms 12:6-7 reminds us the Bible manuscripts have been preserved faithfully, down to our day. And Psalms 119:160 makes it clear inspiration means the information presented is true. Depending on how the original question is asked, one of these secondary verses may actually be a better verse to answer the question!

To make sure these verses are readily available, create a verse list somewhere on the page with the key verse. That is, turn in your Bible to II Timothy 3:16, and then in the margin beside it, print neatly "BIBLE 1". This is the short-cut word, and the question number found on the Bible topics page. Next write your key verse, and then all your secondary references below it. Using the suggested verses above, you would write this in the margin beside II Timothy 3:16.

BIBLE 1
II Timothy 3:16
II Peter 1:21
I Corinthians 2:13
Psalms 12:6-7
Psalms 119:160

If there is not room in the side margin, try writing the verses sideways, running along the margin. Or put the verse list at the top or bottom of the page. Just keep "BIBLE 1" and the key verse there with the verse list, to keep everything connected.

Repeat this process for each of the other questions in your topic.

Once this is finished, you will not only be able to open your Bible to your key verse, but you will be able to find right there on the same page, a list of additional references, to reinforce your answer to whatever question was asked. Even if you don't have those backup verses memorized, you can often remember roughly what they are about and can turn to any of them easily as needed.

Now you know how to add a verse list. Take a few moments today to write in one or more verse lists. If you are using the study guides in our Truth Corps class, you will notice each question begins with a key verse and suggested supplemental verses. Just copy these lists right into your Bible, and you can get your first topic marked in a matter of minutes.

So far so good. You're well on your way to mastering our Cross Reference system. Tomorrow I'll explain how to ramp up your ability to answer questions rapidly. It's an important part of the process. And it's easier than you think. See you then!

Backup Verses
Worksheet

What are some good reasons to have more than one verse prepared to answer a friend's question?

Explain what a "verse list" is, and how it is used in our Bible marking system?

Show what it would look like to write a verse list into your Bible on some specific topic. Feel free to copy the example from today's reading.

Where exactly would you put this verse list in your Bible?

Additional Notes:

Sword Drills
Day 4

    Getting your Bible marked is an important help in being able to answer people's questions. And assuming you have a prepared list of topics, questions, key verses, and verses lists (like the ones in our Truth Corps course), it only takes a quiet afternoon or two to get it entered into your Bible. To use this system skillfully, however, takes a bit of practice. Or as it is sometimes called, sword drills!

    Here are three levels of mastery we encourage you to strive for:

Level One: Key Verse Locations

    While your key verses are all listed on your Bible Topics page, it's far better to turn directly to a key verse without having to look it up. That requires you to remember where your key verses are found. Learning these references has the added advantage of allowing you to answer questions from any Bible, whether it is marked or not. You may not have all your backup verses, but you have at least one verse ready to go.

    In our Truth Corps course, we have 9 topics with 4 or 5 questions each. That comes out to around 40 key verses. With a little work, you can learn all 40 references in as little as a week or two. Not the verse—where it's found.

Here's what we suggest. Get some blank cards (verse cards work fine) and write the question on one side and the key verse on the other. You can use our card generator to create these cards. Then, focus on learning one topic at a time, by doing simple flash card exercises. Look at the question side, try to say the reference, then flip it over and check yourself. Keep at it until you can remember the reference for each question. Add in cards from the next topic, until you know them as well. Then continue until you have learned them all.

Don't rush yourself. Work at it every day, and they will start to stick. Then keep right on reviewing them, to ensure longterm retention. Just like memory verses, having locations instantly accessible requires frequent review. Once you have your key verses memorized you will be able to skip your Bible topics page and go straight to any key verse!

Level Two: Question Variations

Questions don't always come to you exactly as they are worded on your Bible Topics page. In fact, these questions can often be asked in quite a number of ways. For example, questions related to BIBLE 1 about inspiration can take various forms, like: "Aren't there mistakes in the Bible?" "Hasn't the Bible been changed?" "Isn't the Bible out of date?"

Learning to link these questions, with the questions marked in your Bible takes your preparation to the next level. To help with this, simply write out more cards with these question variations on one side of the card, and the key verse on the other. Create as many as you like.

Then practice. Because you already know the references, and the basic questions, they should come quickly. Essentially, you are simply matching each variation to the closest question on your Bible topics page, and then retrieving the key verse you have linked to it. Take a few minutes each day to work through the cards, and you will soon get good at putting the right reference with the question.

It would be easier if these questions always came in the exact same form each time, but they don't. So put a little effort into thinking about the various ways your questions could be asked, and practice connecting them to your key verses. This will help give you the flexibility you need for real life witnessing.

Level Three: Actual Memorization
While it is great to have your Bible marked, and to know where your key verses are found, it is even better to have those verses memorized. Isn't that our ultimate goal? To so fortify our mind with the truths of the Bible, that the Holy Spirit can bring key verses to our remembrance at any time, any place? In fact, memorizing key verses is so powerful, it will enable you to answer questions from God's Word without even having a Bible! For this reason, we recommend eventually memorizing every key verse.

It also is a great help in answering questions that don't fit your normal pattern. Something in the wording of the questions triggers something in your memory and the Holy Spirit is able to bring some verse to mind. You turn to it in your Bible and share the answer. Memorization allows you to search your memory banks by concept, rather than some rigidly worded question, and retrieve the exact verse you need. Combined with ongoing practice, memorization is the ideal way to internalize your key verses.

And it can be done quicker than you think. Work at it little by little. Learn three verses a week and you can easily learn forty in two or three months. Especially if you already know some of them already! But don't stop there - feel free to go on and memorize as many of your secondary verses as you can. The more you know, the more effectively you can answer questions.

For more information about how to memorize, consider taking our FREE Crash Course in Bible memorization. Just visit us at *WWW.FAST.ST/CC*.

All right. You know what to do! Start writing out your questions and key verses on cards and start practicing. Then move on to question variations. And then little by little actual memorization. Before you know it, you will have a sharp sword indeed! Tomorrow we look at how to expand the cross reference system.

Sword Drills
Worksheet

When it comes to knowing where your key verses are found, what are the three levels of mastery we encourage you to pursue:

Level One:

Level Two:

Level Three:

What are two main advantages to learning the references for the keys verses in your chain referencing system?

■

■

What approach is recommended for helping you to learning your key verse references?

Why is it important to add "question variations" into your practice work?

What are the advantages to actually memorizing your key verses?

How long should it take to memorize a few dozen key verses if you work at it steadily?

Additional Notes:

Expanding the System
Day 5

So far we have introduced a basic system of Bible marking designed to help you answer dozens of questions by turning instantly to the exact verse needed, and then providing a short list of great backup verses right there on the same page. While you can use your Bible Topics page in the back of your Bible to look up a key verse, it's better to spend a few weeks memorizing the references of the key verses that go with each question, and then eventually the actual verse. It is a fair bit of work, but it is well worth the effort.

Get your Bible marked, and you'll be glad you did. Our Truth Corps course gives you nine topics with four or five questions each, plus key verses, and verse lists. It will get your cross referencing off to a good start—but it is just that, a start. The Bible has many more topics you will want to eventually mark into your Bible. You may already be thinking of questions or topics you would like to add. Here's how you do it.

First, remember that our Bible marking approach consists of a simple structure built on topics (with a key word), questions (with a key verse), and verse lists. You add to this structure by simply adding new information to the right place in this structure.

Suppose you discover some great verse that reinforces one of the questions already marked in your Bible. Simply turn to the key verse, and add the reference to your verse list. It's as simple as that!

Perhaps one day you will be asked a new question related to some topic marked in your Bible—and your study leads you to a few verses that answer the question. Add that question to your Bible Topics page and choose the key verse that best answers the question. Then, go to that verse, and write in a verse list with the remaining references. Even if its just a couple verses to start with, you can add more later. But don't forget to write out a card for your new question and key verse, and add it to your review drills. Better yet, memorize the verse.

What if you come across a question that is unrelated to any of your current topics? Try to create a broad category for the question. A question on music for example, might go under the category of lifestyle, side by side with questions on entertainment, recreation, appearance, or health, etc. You do not need to have answers to all the questions, or even all the questions at this point, just a broad topic. Choose a key word, and then mark in your first question. You've just begun a new topic!

By wisely adding broad topics, questions, and verse lists, you will soon be able to answer even more of the questions people are asking! Take your time, expand your content carefully, and your ability to answer questions will only improve with time. Your system will take on a life of its own, and grow as you grow.

But remember, practice, practice, practice. Keep up with every question, and every key verse you add.

That's it for today's reading. Tomorrow I want to take a little time to talk about how to answer questions related to so-called problem texts. It's not an easy thing to do, but if you've been keeping up with our instructions so far, you are more than ready for it. Till then...

Expanding the System
Worksheet

How important is it for a cross referencing system to be flexible, and easy to expand?

Explain what you should do when you find a verse that helps answer some question already marked in your Bible.

Explain what you should do when you are confronted with a new question on some topic already marked in your Bible.

Explain what you should do when you come across a question unrelated to any of your current topics.

How important is it continue practicing your "sword drills" as you add new topics, questions, and verses to your chain referencing system?

Additional Notes:

Difficult Questions
Day 6

Congrats on having made it this far in the challenge. If you've been following along carefully, you now know the basic components of our cross referencing system. Using our system of topics, questions, key verses, and verse lists, you can quickly equip yourself to answer dozens of questions—turning instantly in your Bible to the exact answer desired. It takes a bit of time to get your verse lists entered into your Bible, and a bit of practice to learn your key verse locations, but it is definitely doable. And the rewards are worth it.

But the fact is, no amount of preparation will equip you to answer every question. They just won't all fit into nice, neat categories. So what do you do when you get asked a question for which you don't have an answer prepared?

First, don't let this possibility keep you from being willing to talk about what the Bible teaches. The fact is, most people know little about the Bible—and they are unlikely to raise a question beyond the few common ones you will soon have marked in your Bible!

Second, it is helpful to realize you are not responsible to know the answer to every question. It's perfectly fine to say, "I don't know the answer to that, but I'll look into it". In fact, doing this will probably increase your credibility, as you will be seen as humble, genuine, authentic. So relax. Questions you can't answer are fine. Jot their question down on a piece of paper, stick it in your pocket, and don't lose it.

Third, make it a rule to never be caught twice with the same question unprepared. Find a verse or two for each question you can't answer, and add it somewhere to your Bible marking system. And if you can, memorize it too. Review yesterday's reading for tips on how to expand our cross reference system.

Fourth, get back with your friend, and share the verse or two you found that "helped clarify" the question for you. It shows your friend respect to research their question, and then come back with an answer. They will appreciate the effort.

Follow these simple steps consistently, and questions you can't answer will soon become few and far between.

One last thought before closing today's reading: it's a good idea to try and discern whether or not a friend's question is a genuine desire to learn—or instead, a smokescreen. People under conviction sometimes start to raise objections to minor points to evade the consequences of accepting a bigger truth. To debate them in such a situation will only deepen their resistance. If you sense this is what's happening, stay relaxed and friendly. Graciously extend your friend the freedom to interpret Scripture however they choose to. If they are open to it, share the verse you feel best answers their question and then leave the results to God. Give God's Word time to work!

Almost done! Tomorrow is the last day of the challenge, and we've got one last reading you are sure to enjoy! See you there...

Difficult Questions
Worksheet

Despite all your best preparation, how likely is it you will be confronted with a question you can't answer at some point?

Why is this lesson common than most people think?

What should you say (and do) if you don't have a good answer handy? Why will this actually increase your credibility?

What rule should you make, for yourself, related to dealing with difficult questions? What should you do to ensure you stick with that?

How important is it to get back with your friend, and give an answer? What does it show?

Before attempting to answer a friend's questions, what should you try and discern? Why is this important? How should it affect how you answer?

Additional Notes:

Accelerated Sharing
Day 7

Luther's great hymn, A Mighty Fortress, includes this line: "though this world, with devils filled, should threaten to undo us, we will not fear, for God hath willed His truth to triumph through us." And it is true: God's Word will at last accomplish all it has been sent out to do! (Isaiah 55:11).

Before Christ returns, there will be a powerful "refreshing" from "the Lord" which results in a "restitution" of all truths taught in Scripture (Acts 3:19-21). At that time, great power will attend God's people: "Many nations shall come, and say, Come, and let us go up to the mountain of the LORD, and to the house of the God of Jacob; and he will teach us of his ways, and we will walk in his paths: for the law shall go forth of Zion, and the word of the LORD from Jerusalem" (Micah 4:1-2).

Imagine it! Thousands coming into the church from every direction. Why? Because God's Word is going out! From person to person, truth will spread around the globe until the earth is "filled with the knowledge of the glory of the Lord" (Habakkuk 2:14). Truth is going to triumph indeed!

The early church was a powerful, triumphant church, because its members were actively sharing God's Word. The apostles prayed for "all boldness" to "speak thy word" and then gave themselves "continually . . . to the ministry of the word" (Acts 4:29, Acts 6:4). Those they won "went every where preaching the word" (Acts 8:4). "They preached the word of God in the synagogues" to the Jews, and elsewhere to any who "desired to hear the word" (Acts 13:5,7). As a result, "the word of God grew and multiplied" (Acts 12:24). "The word of the Lord was published throughout all the region" (Acts 13:49). And to the very end of the inspired record, they were "teaching and preaching the word of the Lord" "with all confidence, no man forbidding [them]" (Acts 15:35, Acts 28:31). The whole story of Acts is essentially the story of how "the word of God" grew "mightily and prevailed" (Acts 19:20).

There is only one way God's endtime church can experience this New Testament power and fulfil its divine destiny: every member must determine to become a worker.

There is more and more confusion each day about what the Bible really teaches. People everywhere are looking wistfully to heaven for someone to explain its teachings clearly. Thousands are waiting only to be gathered in. But God needs a people He can use to do this exciting endtime work.

Believers who know the truth, must determine to equip themselves to answer questions. By marking their Bibles, learning the locations of key verses, and ultimately memorizing them—they will be fortifying their minds for the exciting times just ahead. They will become instruments God can use at a moment's notice.

But it doesn't stop there. We who are equipped, are exhorted to pass that same training on "to faithful men, who will teach others also" (II Timothy 2:2). It's not enough to mark our Bibles, we must encourage others to mark their Bibles too, and show them how. It's not just "each one reach one", it's "each one teach one". And one way to do that is simply to share this challenge with others. Together we can make a difference! The harvest is plenteous, but the laborers are few. Let's change that! What do you say? The church must rouse to action. It must prepare itself to reach a lost, dying world. Every member must be mobilized for service. Time is short and the work is vast. And what we do, we must do fast...

Accelerated Sharing
Worksheet

What does the Bible prophesy will happen shortly before the return of Christ?

How active was the early church in sharing the Word of God?

Why especially is it important for believers today to equip themselves to share Scripture?

If we are serious about mobilizing an army of workers, what else should we do with this training we have received on Bible marking?

Additional Notes:

FAST Missions
Cutting-Edge Tools and Training

Ready to become a Revival Agent? FAST Missions can help! Our comprehensive training curriculum will give you the skills you need to take in God's Word effectively, live it out practically, and pass it on to others consistently.

Eager to start memorizing God's Word? Our powerful keys will transform your ability to hide Scripture in your heart.

Want to explore the secrets of "real life" discipleship? Our next level training zooms in on critical keys to growth, like Bible study, prayer, time management, and more.

Want to become a worker in the cause of Christ? Our most advanced training is designed to give you the exact ministry skills you need to see revival spread.

For more information, please visit us at:
WWW.FASTMISSIONS.COM

Study Guides

Looking for life-changing study guides to use in your small group or Bible study class? These resources have been used by thousands around the world. You could be next!

Survival Kit
Want to learn how to memorize Scripture effectively? These study guides will teach you 10 keys to memorization, all drawn straight from the Bible. Our most popular course ever!

Basic Training
Discover nuts and bolts keys to the core skills of discipleship: prayer, Bible study, time management, and more. Then learn how to share these skills with others. It is the course that launched our ministry!

Revival Keys
Now as never before, God's people need revival. And these guides can show you how to spark revival in your family, church, and community. A great revival is coming. Are you ready?

Online Classes

Want to try out some of the resources available at FAST? Here is just a small sampling of courses from among dozens of personal and small group study resources:

Crash Course
Discover Bible-based keys to effective memorization.
http://fast.st/cc

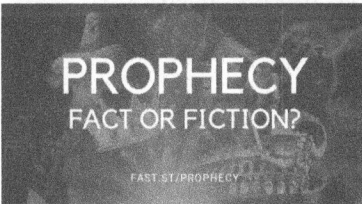

Fact or Fiction
Does the Bible really predict future events? You be the judge.
http://fast.st/prophecy

Monkey Business
Find out how evolution flunks the science test.
http://fast.st/monkey

Revive
Want more of God's Spirit? Learn how to pursue revival.
http://fast.st/revive

The Lost Art
Rediscover New Testament keys to making disciples.
http://fast.st/lostart

Digital Tools

FAST offers a number of powerful "apps for the soul" you can use to grow in your walk with God. And many of these are completely free to anyone with an account. Some of these include:

Review Engine
Our powerful review engine is designed to help ensure effective longterm Bible memorization. Give it a try, it works!

Bible Reading
An innovative Bible reading tool to help you read through the entire Bible, at your own pace, and in any order you want.

Prayer Journal
Use this tool to organize important requests, and we'll remind you to pray for them on the schedule you want.

Time Management
Learn how to be more productive, by keeping track of what you need to do and when. Just log in daily and get stuff done.

For more information about more than twenty tools like these, please visit us at *http://fast.st/tools*.

Books

If the content of this little book stirred your heart, look for these titles by the same author.

For Such A Time...
A challenging look at the importance of memorization for the last days, including topics such as the Three Angel's messages and the Latter Rain.

Moral Machinery
Discover how our spiritual, mental, and physical faculties work together using the sanctuary as a blueprint. Astonishing insights that could revolutionize your life!

The Movement
Discover God's plan to finish the work through a powerful endtime movement. Gain critical insights into what lies just ahead for the remnant!